DREAMS I NEVER TOLD YOU
&
LETTERS I NEVER SENT

DREAMS I NEVER TOLD YOU
&
LETTERS I NEVER SENT

POEMS BY DAVID WOJCIECHOWSKI

Gold Wake

I was dreamin' when I wrote this, forgive me if
it goes astray

— Prince Roger Nelson, "1999"

I'm tired.

When the birds stop

I will wake up or not.

The windows are open.

— Joseph Ceravolo, "Noise Outside"

CONTENTS

I

II

III

I

In this dream I'm running a dream farm and glue
 factory.

Dreams run everywhere.

Even into the glue factory.

One dream is on fire.

This dream burns down the farm, the factory.

The whole site is smoldering.

People smell it from miles away.

They wander wafting air.

They show up with graham crackers, marshmallows,

dreams of chocolate.

You wake into darkness but you hear the horse.

The horse is there to ground you.

Without it   just the darkness

The uncertainty of the darkness   if it's around

Or in you. But there's that warm exhalation.   In the
     real

Darkness you can almost see it from the nostrils.

There's the click of the tapping hoof. The clatter of the
     skeletal horse song.

That song reminds you of when you fell asleep in the
     darkness.

When you probably entered it tied to something.

You reach toward the heavy breathing of a horse.

You can't find it. You hear it, but you can't find it.

It has to be out there. The sound is just out there. Just
     there.

Forward, forward, forward. Follow the clattering.

Follow the sweet-boned voice.   Until it's time for bed.

The apples fall into black waters.

The rain never quite begins. It just was.

Can't end without a beginning.

Those apples are gone. The trees

Are next. I wipe the mud from the streets

I mean the mud from my feet,

On the mat, covered in more mud.

I splash into the house. Wonder

How the cats are doing in all of this.

An apple floats by. A package of

Grocery store cookies. "This won't stop," says

Someone I assume to be the grocery clerk.

"Can't stop. Didn't start," I might have

Replied. The water levels out to ankle depth

As the house breaks and follows along

The path of the apple and I think of anchors.

But it's a house. And there's no water.

Cause it's not raining. So this house isn't floating

Away. It's not going to collect in some place

With all of the others.

WHEN SOMEONE DIES
I AM LESS CONFUSED

Only because there is more oxygen

in my immediate future.

Depending on closeness

time increases, as the space between us

stretches—get it?

That's what the whole thing is doing.

Moving away from itself.

Think of any cartoon where the bunny

divides itself in half.

To get around a tree

or to avoid a circular saw in a log factory,

or maybe it was the coyote divided in half by the bird.

Either way you know

How it is to move away from the thing you are.

You've seen how the car goes right through,

or the tree passes and then

there's the meeting. But not here.

That's not what would happen

If the cartoon continued.

If that bunny went around the tree

and came back on the other side and continued

going on. Living his cartoon bunny life.

Things would separate. The self would keep dividing
as space grows.
As the air increases and the bunny breathes more—
both lungs on either side of a tree,
Either side of a saw, either side of a ray
gun/axe/roadrunner/rocket/boobytrap—
It's because there's less to need air
and there's more room to put it all.
The bunny will be pulled away from itself,
but so will the tree,
and everything else.

I THOUGHT YOU WROTE *WORLDS* NOT *WORDS*

You wanted us to take the planets apart.
So it's what I'm trying to do.
As many as I can grab in a fist. Like gumballs.
I sprint through the void with my hands out.
Grabbing wildly. Twisting them until they are
Two and letting them whirl back into nothing.
Watch as I dash with my hands splayed.
Watch as a planet catches under my sole.
Watch as I splay out into the black.

THE MIRROR SAID YES
BUT GIVE ME A FEW DAYS

And so I did
I waited and the webs gathered
Gathered more than one would expect.
Kind of a cocoon of them.
A livable cocoon. One with halls—narrow
And oddly shaped, but that is the nature
Of a webbed-in house.

There are the things that are in the house.
Once a table, now more of a white mound.
I haven't seen my shoes in days, and I've
Given up on socks.

When I breathe out I get the feeling that
I'm seeing webs in the air.

They fall gently. Become more of the floor.
I've taken to hunching as it rises.
I'll be hunched on all fours soon.
My fingers guiding me through my home.

YOU WILL PAINT THEM IN COLORS
THAT WERE NOT THERE

Because there is no color for clear just a child's sky blue
    crayon when trying to say this, this is my house

And this is the perpetual smoke from the fire we burn
    year-round despite the sun being out

Despite the leaves on the tree in what must be a yard
    next to this house that is green

I only had the one green crayon so I guess the house too
    looks leaf-covered, leaf-ful,

Choked from the inside or sea sick and turning green
    or, conversely, the tree is aluminum siding

And functions as a small round house in itself and
    sometimes it's where we live perhaps

this is not our house, this is just leaf and sky and smoke
    and fire

THE WIND CALMLY DIES
ON AN EMPTY BOTTLE

One last *shink* of life before there's nothing
Just a sparkle in the distance
Everything far away
And you remember the feeling of that night
Still maybe this night the air

It came here to rest finally

One last mark in history
Even if it's not important
You want to borrow the vase
You want the whole thing, flowers, water, all
Just to borrow
You'll return it when you're done
And you never say why

You return years later

How did you do this?

And I open my mouth

Pull out more flowers

And more flowers

And more flowers throwing

All manner of flowers on the ground

Until I find a few more just like the ones from earlier

I throw them up

SHADOW OF A BICYCLE: NOW THERE'S A CARD

For me it's on the wall, a slight shift to the shadow,
But there is no bike. Not in this version.
Can't say for certain where it's gone.
Ridden off home, or to another one, left and forgotten
And taken, rolled away on its own.
There's no bike. The shadow. The wall is
Still the wall itself. Solid, with a shadow on it.

From the deck you deal four cards. Three friends.
They each turn over the usual. Something red
Or black. A figure or some symbols.
You turn over yours, and it's a shadow
Of a bicycle. The silhouette of movement's
Potential. Your friends shift in their seats and one
By one get up to go. You go outside
With your card and put it in the spokes of
Your own bike, and you wheel it off down
The hill toward the town hoping it steadies itself
Long enough for you to hear the *fwip fwip fwip*
Turn into air.

DID NOT SO MUCH LIVE
UPON THIS ISLAND

In space you like to float

Think it's what you do out there in black excess

   sprinkled with light

Does it feel dark like a closed room

Or do you know it's all out there

I guess I want to experience true outside dark

Without a star for reference

Just shadows of trees—I hope

The grass grows up to strangle my feet

Sticking me to a spot

And I wave arms out in front of me

Sides

Back

Nothing but nothing but air and dark

No light

Lack of clouds but stars too or are the clouds as dark as

   all of this

I guess the area doesn't exist now

Except for my being there in it

But these are intangible, lazy things

I'm lost out here so I'll think

NO CLEAR WATER IN THOSE EYES

Instead there's something murky, pond scum, or silt
Clouds scuttled up by the passing of itself
It's the way disappearing works
To think of a thing that exists in itself. Passes itself.
Reacts in and of itself and then can disappear into itself,
or forever, whichever way it wants it to be but now I no
longer remember which is which.

I could break into a million pieces. I could be a
lumberjack. I could plant trees. I could be a tree
shepherd. A wolf in trees' clothing. Bark for skin. Peeling
off layers to the center. Writing on myself or building a
house out of myself perhaps throwing myself into a fire
to keep me warm—oh the wonderful things I could do
to me if I were a tree.

THE ACCIDENTS
WILL BE KINDER THAN US.

Elephant ears are a way of predicting your death.

Climb inside, curl into it, pull it over you,

A cracked, dirt-grey sleeping sack

And you count the hours you sleep.

Did you dream? If it was about water, that's important.

If you were an animal, that's a different important.

I tried it and had night sweats.

Woke up hot, couldn't unravel the elephant

Or I'd be too cold. There's a moon out tonight.

There's more than a moon out tonight.

Some of them blink. Some of the moons

I mean.

BUT THE HOUSE WE ENTER GIVES
EACH OF US A LANGUAGE

There are crickets in the stairs
And I will never find them

I'm missing too many of the little things
Worlds and moons and water and fish

Think of the boat you once abandoned
Think of the time you sank to the bottom

And never rose again

Think of the millions of bubbles you saw down there

You made a world down there
You piled sand into intricate if not unsteady walls

You kept to these walls, these walls without roof
When does your sand house simply resemble a crater?

A home with too much water, a home with too many
  stars

I SAY GOODNIGHT
FROM BEHIND A CORNER

And then turn into building, huddle into my coat, and
pretend you don't see me.

But of course you do. Of course you see me. I'm right
there, under my coat.

You can hear me breathing. You see a little of my
breathing. The coat falls. The air rises.

It's this way of not letting on that I've forgotten how to
leave. Or how to get around a wall.

How to pass through matter. Easy, you think, but, here
I am against the wall. Shrouded.

Then I'm not in the coat. I realize this after a while I'm
behind me huddling in the coat.

Or rather I don't think I'm in there. I'm behind. The
coat is empty. It's a shell. And I've become my breath.

Not my breath, but the everything around it. The
everything around my coat. I've swallowed the coat
and keep expanding.

Soon I'm larger than I realize. Soon the city is gone.
Soon I am rivers. Soon I am trees and cars and hot
dog stands and some playgrounds. Soon I am houses
where other people grew up in. Sooner than I realize
I'm telephone poles. I'm atmosphere. I'm the internet.

I end it when I become the moon and decide *this*.
This is the one to stay. Releasing everything else the
coat falls to the ground next to the building.
You look up and there are few stars. There's a moon.
It's night now. You don't know when that happened.

II

Dear you,

When the curtain opens on the yard, the house is the background. You will wait for the hands like the rest of us. You with little choice, you are paralyzed without them. Me, I'm there too. I have the choice to move, I'm not part of your production. I was an innocent enough bystander until I slipped backstage. I tripped over the prop sprinkler, clunked my skull on the prop gnome, and now I'm here. In the house on the couch—wondering— if I do have that choice I spoke of earlier.

Dear you,

Once, as a smaller boy, I poured honey all over my yard. My parent's yard and mine. I drenched it: the money shot of yard honey.

I took my parents, by the pant leg or skirt, to the window and raised my hands like miniature Moses. I said, *Look. Life.*

Dear you,

That's the big secret no one wants us to know; flight isn't just something the birds can do. Flight is hidden inside the birds themselves. Lightness. It's the bones. They're not hollow as we learn in second grade science (they keep this from us for a reason), but the bones of a bird are filled with sky. You have to catch the smallest ones, for their bones contain the most sky. Curious, isn't it? But you must crack the bones in one motion and quickly suck from them the sky. Then you'll float. You'll grow wings. Your bones will in turn fill with sky. Your marrow turns blue in the day, black at night—it shines with stars, swims with clouds. This can be beautiful, but it will be dangerous, as now you can never land without the weight of your body crushing the very frame that lifted you up.

Dear you,

In a book I'm reading there's a story of man's first spaceward movement. The NASA think tanks got it into their heads that ants were the key to man's survival. They made suits out of ants. Helmets out of ants. O2 masks out of ants. And when they shimmied through atmo—those ants began to explode.

Up there, if you squint tight, I bet birds look a lot like dying stars blinking in and out.

Dear you,

I'm sorry about your elephant, even though, in all honesty, I think you're making it up. I think it's all bullshit because you move so quickly from the elephant to your hand. You wanted to see this creature. You traveled so far to see this creature. Do you understand the size of an elephant? If you were there with one, did you not feel small? Did you not feel soft? To save the elephant, you have to go tit for tit and tat for tat. I saved an elephant once. I hacked off my legs and my less dominant arm and most of the forearm on the remainder. This stump pulled me, ground trench, to the elephant where I made an opening in its chest big enough for part of a man—because I was now part of a man. I crawled inside to the cardiac pocket, wound arteries around and through my meager appendages, and in a baritone I did my best *thump thump, thump thump.* Is it working? Is the elephant still alive?

Dear you,

This is regarding the idea of grinding bones to make bread: how? Do you have instructions? I like to bake and fear I'll soon have nothing left to work with. With which to work.

I have a mortar and pestle. Is that a start? I'll start.

Dear you,

Last night was the giant's birthday. The party. I wasn't necessarily invited, nor did I intend to go, but I was out for a walk and I became the entertainment. Out in what I thought were the woods gone waxy, a firestorm came from the sky. Blazes ignited the trees and I ran, slipshod, through mud and fire, then a gust of wind took it all away. The fire was gone, my ears echoed, and then I saw a giant glinting moon shard coming down from the sky, almost like a knife into cake.

Dear you,

My grandfather used to tell me about a time on his farm when the cows started giving dirt. Instead of milk, they produced dirt. Pure earth. I remember just thinking *how awful for the cows.* But then I thought *what if those cows had secrets and now the secrets have no milk to feed on?* Just think. Think of all those emaciated secrets. Limping and exhausted. Shards of mental glass. How awful.

Dear you,

It's a circular cloud in your vision, something perfect but being pulled apart. In my fifth grade science book, I learn that below the clouds are *arbor, escarpments, canis latrans*, even my face, which gives way to its own kind of avalanche. One where instead of rocks and a rush of snow, my face just topples over itself until it arrives safely on the ground, where it will be covered and put to bed. *It prays about fear and darkness and the earth*, you say to the Ashman, the impish shadow spirit of it all, sitting in the chair in the corner, pulling apart grey night clouds.

Dear you,

Today I purchased new eyes from the antique shop. They allow me to look back through myself. They allow me to look back through everything.

I write this letter with bone. I sit in the soft blades of dirt and stone.

I can almost feel my stomach lurch toward my chest when I realize my hands are both there and not there— both holding the paper and letting the wind take it—but my stomach and chest are experiencing the same uncertain reality. Wherever these eyes are showing me, I just see wind and faint phantoms of everything I'm going to do or everything I've already done.

Dear you,

Earlier today I was chewing on the sky. Letting it drip on to my shirt. My shirt soaked in sky. Eventually my body just tapered off into nothing. I started offering people wishes but never really fulfilling them. I'm not really a genie, just a man disappearing. I still granted them hope if you think about it. Except you. I'm granting your wish. Here's that gray box full of styrofoam and a shattered bottle. There's also a note in there from me. It's this one.

Dear you,

This is the way puppets come to be. It's not always interesting—bits of wood, some felt, strings and it's happening. But there are those *bullish* puppets where wood won't do (*Splinter Life* they call it). These are the puppets that have mannequinean dreams. They want that full self-power and the chance to regard things as lower than them. They will slouch in theater shadows, a lit match burning down to their fingers. They absorb it thinking someday their hollow face will appear on the newsstand surrounded by friends.

Dear you,

It can't be said this carpet had intent to peel up this way—there's cement below it, seemingly cave-like, and I've come to trace crude creatures more and more on your face and body. I bestow upon you a history, part make-believe, the other part is my brain wracked in torchlight. The rest of me is coming off, forming a thin film over everything in this cave. Even sound, the snores of what I've come to find as my inspiration, a bear. When I peel back its fur, there's not bear beneath, but wood. A large boat I climb into as I scratch waves into you and flood the cave. I lay down in the boat and trace raw voyagers onto you. This isn't art. This is a boat that was a bear that came out of a cave and is slowly sailing beyond.

Dear you,

I thought you said this is *bread* humor and I left for the corner store to see if you were lying. I was killing in the aisle. Then I took a few slices out for drinks. It was raining, and I quickly lost them. I mean lost them like a doctor pounding a chest and yelling clear. I haven't been funny since. I have dreams I'm getting warmer. I'm getting too warm. Suddenly I'm dried up and burnt, and I'm being thrown to the pigs.

Dear you,

When I open my mouth birdsong comes out. There's a
nest there, I swallowed it ages ago, on a dare. I must have
been 8. I was double-dogged. So I swallowed the nest,
and I never spoke again.

Dear you,

The mountain is engulfed in flames. The great mountain we can't see beyond. My wife spent the last four days staring into the mountain fire. This morning I woke up, there was smoke above my bed. My wife is missing. The bed is unsinged. There's no ash. Just the smoke that I might have married drifting along the ceiling.

III

AND ALL THAT LIGHT SHOUTED

And all that light shouted
At once and then was gone
The air floats with filaments
And then there you are,
In the background, defected
Skirting the responsibilities of history
Like the dark can live in itself
Or the way a man rides a horse
At night, and you
Sink these many
Glowing orbs just off shore
And watch until they are gone
Like the ocean is swallowing the stars
And for a second you go mad—
Diving down to retrieve them

DRIFTING LIKE SPIRITS

We have a natural tendency toward drift,
And we open the windows and doors of the house
And float right through.
The front door comes, and the back door goes.
We lose ourselves really far away from home.
There are ways to sink. You developed
Them with rocks and pockets, but
You go from drift to drag. Example:
The boat is leaving, the people are happy and wave,
But then the boat's on land, and they have to stay.

UNFINISHED SPIRIT HAND

My hand fell off in my head.

I took my wrist for granted.

Never again. Now we all know

The dangers behind

The brain. Botany is a success,

A way of disallowing death access—

But that's getting too baldly philosophic.

I made a new hand out of spirits

I plucked from the airs.

This hand glowed, hearts in

It beating until I

Lost track of my own.

This hand can touch hot rails,

Moves through the faces

It tries to remember, precisely.

It looks like fireflies or moths or particles

Or constellations that got too clustered.

Where did you go, little ghost, where are you?

Washing my hand in a stream

It dissipates from within

Becomes more hollow, not.

FARM ARMS

I got my arms stuck in the soil at the farm.
Leaning too far forward, I was sucked down toward
The ground. I'm not positive what is taking root, only
The rest of me spends my time in this groove between
Rows of vegetables, in the metallic shade and sun of this
    tractor.

In time there will have to be something to harvest.
Children
Will tell stories about the plant-man living in the field.
This is how they will trick one another into being good.
This is how I will become forgotten and remembered.
This version, the children-made me out of words,
And the real me are disappearing into the darkness
Of towering crops.

NO TIME FOR NIGHT

This is the thought
that will keep me
whole, more or less
And when time comes around
the sky will not
allow room
for birds and what
they want
That's truth in time
Forward and back
See something
Say something
A void that's
falling into its self
Become the queen
of nothing
Swim into air
Doors look admiringly on you
You swore there'd be
no weather
today
But there is

COLOR TIN

On the table I've placed some items.
They all fit into this small tin I carry.
It's not important that I tell you
What the items are. Let's just say
They are colors that came too late
To this world. I've had them all my life.
Ever since I first left that oak ship.
Things were grayer than they are
Now. The oak was by a lake and the lake
Was gray. I found the tin at that lake bottom. Now
That's where I sit, opening and closing the tin,
Arranging and rearranging the colors on this large flat
   rock
That I call the table.

A MAN AND A BEAR
WAIT FOR THE MAIL

The day begins to open into morning.

The world is a trance.

There's a man, he's hoping for a newspaper.

There's a bear, he's hoping for a fish.

In the mail that day,

They will both learn their brothers are dead.

The morning is closing in

On the array of colors

That drip into this day.

The tan of a fence. The red of a chimney.

The dull grey of ropes.

The man pretends to not see

The letter/the bear, yet.

He takes one step into air, curling

his body into the sky.

The bear sees this too.

YOUR CHILDHOOD ON THE PHONE

Your childhood is on the phone, calling again.
The cord trips through mounds you built on the shore,
Steps from the water, hoping for a moat.
You can't help but slip back into this time.
There was a building leading up to the shore. In this
Building, you were expected to change. We got there in
  the mornings
And by the early afternoon, it was lunch and games for
  a quarter.

I'm standing in the Laundromat, at a claw machine,
  trying to get a stuffed elephant. For us.
I don't lose. I win every
Time. There's probably a camera somewhere here.
Every triumph, every tumbling stuffed victory recorded.
In my memory now, this tape is playing
Away and away into the dawn.
It's a fanciful notion, freeing all these creatures from
  their glass box with a metal claw/a metal selection.
I arrange them in a circle and we have tea.
I'm 30 years old. I pass the sugar.
The elephant reaches for it.

YEARS AND BAGS

How many years and bags will it take before we come to
    this—
All of us are now trees.

We have a future made of wooden boats, and we aim
    for the end:
The edge. We aim for faded light.
We drop days into waters.

I like to visit the Sky and ask him what his plans are but
he tells me he only has the one and we are supposed to
recognize it when we see it but I don't believe in things
that way so I carve my initials into the wall behind the
bookcase and when I come back I'll look for them just to
make sure the fading light doesn't move, and the end will
always be here, and there will be a wooden dock, full of
wooden boats, made from trees, that used to be us.

THEN TOWN

I filled my hills with music
And under the streets
I filled every square inch with mirrors
And sound and image repeated forever after.

I grew bored then
Having accomplished my trick of tones
And repetitions. I decided to peek
Into the book of marionettes.

There I found ways of washing
The world I created: bats, wind, lakes,
String and wood.

I paused for the exact time it
Took for the waves of nostalgia
To crush this world I founded,
This town that was.

MY HEAD IS NOW AN AQUARIUM

When they moved into my house, they showed me
    what a wonderful aquarium my skull could be.

A spot was cut for me in the wall, so I would be
    unobtrusive, part of the décor, and the people took
    turns

Sliding me out of the wall a few inches, feeding the
    fish.

They threw parties

And the guests were told to not tap on the glass. My
    face is now glass. This

is what I do now. I house fish.

It got to a point where I took a certain pride in my
    position, my ego grew large and soon schools

Could be seen in the deepest reaches of my skull. There
    were trenches that, at best,

Someone in an old 1800's copper helmet might skim
    the surface of, not so much diving,

But falling, aiming for the darkest parts, bubbles
    suspended behind him during his fall.

NEIGHBORING CLOUDS

Clouds make poor neighbors
As I'm constantly yelling *fire*
Only to have the firemen show up
Disappointed

I'm waiting for the other—
I'm going away
You want to settle this now
So I dig through the attic looking for the telescope

Stars tonight make mundane constellations
The Settee, The Ladle, The German Shepherd
I find one close to me, very near
And I hold my hand out for fun

These things—
They burn   This is why things crash into the land
And call themselves *at home*
As they explode ahead of their own being

I wake up in a room
Looking over

The sky is in a chair, stone faced
All of it—night, day, storm, clear, shimmered or blue

And therein, nobody
Knows that when I start yelling *fire*
I'm really yelling for light, I'm yelling back
Into drifting smoke

WE FORM A SINGLE WORD

We empty ourselves into homes
It's an effort to travel
And when we do we're lost in trees
There is light looking for us
All it finds is the smoke
Of where we've been, a past-place

We sink into water to grow smaller
All of those bubbles are the lucky ones
We creep along, slow moving sand
Skeletons of men
We always forget there were others
And each of them had their own methods
For being saved

DREAMS I NEVER TOLD YOU
&
LETTERS I NEVER SENT

ACKNOWLEDGMENTS

Some of these poems have appeared in *Better, Heavy Feather Review, Horse Less Review* and *Spork*, and I am very grateful to those editors for supporting my work. Various titles in section one are borrowed lines from Michael Burkard's selected poems, *Envelope of Night.*

I'd like to thank Chris for first telling me these poems were a book. Thanks to Kyle for helping me shape them into a real live book and to Nick for making it shine. I would also like to thank everyone who has helped me with these poems and has encouraged my writing over the years, specifically: Michael, Taylor, Erin, Lindsay, Bruce, and, of course, my father who supported my writing from the beginning.

ABOUT GOLD WAKE PRESS

Gold Wake Press, an independent publisher, is curated by Nick Courtright and Kyle McCord. All Gold Wake titles are available at amazon.com, barnesandnoble.com, and via order from your local bookstore. Learn more at goldwake.com. Available Titles:

Kelly Magee's *The Neighborhood*
Keith Montesano's *Housefire Elegies*
Kyle Flak's *I am Sorry for Everything in the Whole
        Entire Universe*
Joshua Butts' *New to the Lost Coast*
Mary Buchinger Bodwell's *Aerialist*
Becca J. R. Lachman's *Other Acreage*
Lesley Jenike's *Holy Island*
Tasha Cotter's *Some Churches*
Nick Courtright's *Let There Be Light*
Kyle McCord's *You Are Indeed an Elk, But This is
        Not the Forest You Were Born to Graze*
Hannah Stephenson's *In the Kettle, the Shriek*
Kathleen Rooney's *Robinson Alone*
Erin Elizabeth Smith's *The Naming of Strays*

ABOUT THE POET

David Wojciechowski's poems have appeared in *Bateau,
Better, iO,* and *Meridian* among others. A founding
editor of *NightBlock,* David is a freelance designer and
editor, and he teaches writing and literature at various
colleges. He can be found at www.davidwojo.com and
elsewhere.

CPSIA information can be obtained
at www.ICGtesting.com
Printed in the USA
FFOW04n2045181116
29449FF